BOETHIUS

The Consolation of Philosophy

Edited and abridged by
JAMES J. BUCHANAN
Princeton University

With an Introduction by
WHITNEY J. OATES
Princeton University

UNGAR • NEW YORK

MILESTONES
OF THOUGHT
in the History of Ideas

General Editor
F. W. STROTHMANN
Stanford University

Eighth Printing, 1987

ISBN 0-8044-6057-4

Copyright 1957 by
Frederick Ungar Publishing Co.

Printed in the United States of America

Library of Congress Catalog Card Number: 57-8649

[handwritten annotations: "why in jail — stood up for other senators in conspiracy" / "He may have taken bribes." / "He says in jail because of beliefs"]

INTRODUCTION

One of the most remarkable documents to come out of Classical Antiquity is Boethius' *Consolation of Philosophy*. The author's life (480-524 A.D.) falls at the very end of the ancient classical world, and indeed there are many who would urge that at this time Greco-Roman culture in any meaningful sense of the term had ceased to exist. Such a view is extreme, for although the level of culture had sunk disastrously at the end of the fifth century, there still were many significant vestiges, in Italy at least, of the great Roman past. The rulers now in the Eternal City were of barbarian stock, and it was Theodoric the Great, the King of the Ostrogoths, who became the Roman Emperor in 493 A.D. Many curious elements were combined in the polity of Theodoric. First, there were the remnants of the old Roman order: the Senate, the consuls, and other traditional officials plus a theoretic adherence to the Roman Empire of the East. Add to these a strong strain of Gothic barbarism, along with the institution of the Church, the orthodox form of which was in virtually continuous conflict with threatening heresy. The political significance of these ecclesiastical quarrels can be readily seen in the fact that Theodoric himself was a fierce proponent of the Arian heresy, whereas Justin, his opposite number as the Emperor of Constantinople, adhered to orthodoxy. And in all this curious political, cultural, and religious amalgam at its pivotal point stood the enigmatic Theodoric himself. He genuinely wanted to fuse the Roman and the Gothic, for, unlike some other barbarian invaders, he had come to Italy to stay and not as a transient in search of loot. He recognized the superiority of Roman culture and desired to preserve some elements within it, but for all his respect for Roman law, order, and good government he was not able to restrain his own inherent cruelty and brutality.

This was the age into which Boethius was born. It is all the more astonishing to find in him, a member of a noble Roman family which had been Christian since the time of Constantine, a man of supreme cultivation. He possessed at once a sensitive mind, great literary and poetic powers, scholarly attainments, and philosophic insight. As a young scholar he set himself the stupendous task of translating the entire works of Plato and Aristotle into Latin (thus bespeaking the disappearance of Greek in the Italy of that period) and as part of his project, by commentary and tract, he hoped to reconcile the differences between these two masters of ancient thought. He did not complete this undertaking, but, considering his active participation in public life, he accomplished much. He rendered into Latin the *Organon* of Aristotle along with extensive commentary, and in addition wrote several treatises on logic, music, and arithmetic, as well as the famous theological *Tractates* and the supreme gem, *The Consolation of Philosophy*.

Like St. Augustine, Boethius was able to produce this extraordinary volume of writing and at the same time be absorbed in a life of exacting activity. At the age of thirty (it is hard to believe that he died at forty-four) he became a consul. He enjoyed the high favor of Theodoric, as is evidenced by the fact that his two sons were appointed consuls in the same year, 522 A.D. Boethius' political power reached its zenith when he held the post of *Magister Officiorum*, in which he functioned virtually as the Emperor's prime minister. Then, with crashing suddenness, fortune changed. Boethius was arrested for treason, imprisoned, condemned without trial, and tortured to death. Why this happened we shall probably never know. Some have maintained that when Theodoric unjustly accused some members of the Senate of conspiracy, Boethius rushed to their defense in a spirit of upholding senatorial dignity and as a result was taken into custody. Others have sought an explanation in a supposed conflict between the Arian Theodoric and the orthodox Boethius. At all events, the

Christian scholar, Boethius, found himself imprisoned, without his precious library, awaiting execution, and from this situation *The Consolation of Philosophy* was born.

The *Tractates* of Boethius exhibit unusual competence in the field of Christian theology and they are infused with the spirit of deep Christian conviction. In contrast, the *Consolatio* contains no specific reference to Christianity but rather expresses a lofty "natural theology" written in the spirit of Greek philosophy. Some have wondered why in his extreme of despair, his "moment of truth," he turned for comfort not to religion but to philosophy. It is perhaps valid to conjecture that, as both a philosophical and a religious scholar, Boethius, in anticipation of the later scholastic writers, drew the distinction between faith and reason. Perhaps, as he faced his execution, he sought and found his greatest solace in building a case for his religion, Christianity, by invoking the instrument of reason without appeal to the data of revelation or faith. In so doing he made the most of the Greek tradition he loved in his effort to reinforce his Christian faith. Certainly there is nothing in the tone and feeling of the *Consolatio* which could be called non-Christian, yet its reliance so exclusively upon the tradition of Greek philosophy makes it in effect the last document of Classical Antiquity.

The *Consolatio* is written in an ancient form known as the Menippean satire, that is, in alternating sections of prose and poetry. Since the accompanying translation is in prose, it may be difficult to distinguish the prose sections from the poetic in the original Latin. Suffice it to say that the poetic passages serve to sum up the argument and to mark pauses while Boethius reflects upon the position he has reached. Philosophically, the work reveals great indebtedness to Plato, Aristotle, the Stoics, and Plotinus, but especially and primarily to Plato. In fact, the late Professor E. K. Rand has called Boethius the greatest Platonist in antiquity. Written as a dialogue between Boethius in prison and the personified Lady Philosophy, the *Consolatio* opens with an apology for the writer's career and his thoughts on the vagaries of Fortune. Thereafter the founding questions which beset all men are treated: the moral government of the universe, the problem of evil, the dilemma posed by the notion of man's free will as against God's foreknowledge, the meaning of eternal life, and the nature of human happiness. This is but a brief glimpse of the scope and range of the work. Its influence was vast, for up to the recovery of the Classics in the Renaissance, it was one of the few sources of information for the Greek tradition. It has always been famous and has been often translated and imitated. Notable among the translations are those of King Alfred (*ca.* 890 A.D.) and of Queen Elizabeth I.

In considering Boethius' philosophical position, one is struck by his treatment of the question of evil. From one point of view his attitude coincides with that of the Stoics, *viz.*, there is no intrinsic evil in the Universe. In some measure this position is fused with the view of the Neo-Platonists and of St. Augustine, to the effect that becoming evil involves a lessening of existence, since only Good exists in the full sense of the word. In this connection, Boethius raises the question of the prosperity of the wicked and the misfortune of good men. The answer is given by Lady Philosophy (Book IV, Prose 2f.). The argument is really a reprise of certain sections of Plato's *Gorgias* and may be summarized in some such terms as these: What does one mean by power? Take the case of a tyrant. Is he happy? Does he do exactly what he wants to do? In the eyes of the world, he does. But actually man can only want or wish or desire the good. If what he does is not good, he does what he does not wish to and hence has no real power. He is merely mistaken. Evils arise from men in their ignorance supposing that they can do—or have the power to do— what they will, whereas they really have *power*, in the proper understanding of the term, only to do good—only to *will* the good.

There is no need to dwell upon the attitude of Boethius towards earthly possessions and their vanity. (Much of Boethius' discussion of this question has been omitted from the present text.) It is enough to point out that his is the typical *contemptio mundi* so characteristic of ancient thought. He insists that it is folly to be subservient to Fortune and her whims. He exhorts us to remember that God governs the Universe, and therefore the total effect must be good. Ill fortune, so-called, has its disciplinary power. Since God is supreme in the Universe, it is folly to set up Fortune as a goddess. The famous lines of Juvenal (X. 365-366) come to mind: "Thou wouldst have no divinity, O Fortune, if we had but wisdom; it is we that make a goddess of thee, and place thee in the skies."

Most important of all in Boethius' thought is his approach to the problem of Free Will and Providence. His attack begins by picking up the distinction between time and eternity first enunciated by Plato in the *Timaeus*, and subsequently invoked by Plotinus and St. Augustine. Though the distinction is old, it seems clear that Boethius was original in the way in which he employed it in order to throw light upon the problem of the Freedom of the Will. In the fifth Book of the *Consolatio*, the author analyzes the question by asking how free is man if God knows in advance all we will do and choose. Boethius attempts to solve this dilemma by considering the implications of God's eternal existence. If He is eternal, then all events, past, present, and future, must be in his awareness all at once. In other words, so it is contended, just as the events we see happening in our own present and presence are not made necessary or unnecessary by the fact that we observe them, so the things which God observes are not determined by the fact that He who sees all time as one eternal present knows them—from our point of view—"in advance."

The nature of this view and the argument on its behalf bears further elaboration in the following four points:

1. God is eternal, and this quality in Him (the divine Eternity) reveals—in so far as it can be revealed—the nature of the Divine Knowledge.

2. Since God is eternal, His knowledge is not conditioned, as man's is, by time. Instead, He has "all at once complete and perfect possession of unlimited life." (Book V, Prose 6).

3. What for man is successive, is for God simultaneous, that is, what man experiences as past, present, and future, lies unrolled before God as a changeless eternal present.

4. From this comes the answer to the old question, "Can man be free if God knows all?" God's seeing as present what for man is yet to come does not impose necessity on the event any more than does our sight of present acts place constraint on them. If man was created by God a free agent, then man's free acts do not become unfree by God's knowledge, which is properly called not "pre-vision" but Providence. It is not awareness of something future, but sure knowledge of a timeless moment that never passes. God's outlook, or looking forth, embraces all things, as from some lofty height.

Such then in brief outline is the position of Boethius. His life and writings, coming as they do from this dismal, barbaric epoch of history, are doubly impressive, for they lead us to believe that no matter how bad the external circumstances, man at his best can do great things. Of one thing more we can be sure: Boethius' vision of man's nature and his relation to God and the Universe will always endure as one of the noblest products of the human mind.

WHITNEY J. OATES

SELECTED BIBLIOGRAPHY

Barrett, H. M. *Boethius: Some Aspects of His Times and Work*. Cambridge, 1940.

Patch, H. R. *The Tradition of Boethius: A Study of His Importance in Medieval Culture*. New York, 1935.

Rand, E. K. "On the Composition of Boethius' *Consolatio Philosophiae*." *Harvard Studies in Classical Philology XV*, 1904, pp. 1ff.

Stewart, A. F. and Rand, E. K. *Boethius*. The Loeb Classical Library. Harvard University Press, 1918.

Stewart, H. F. *Boethius: An Essay*. Edinburgh, 1891.

NOTE

The present edition is based in part on Cooper's translation, which has, however, undergone a complete review and a thorough overhauling. In addition, to meet the requirements of this Series, the work has been abridged. Where abridgments have been made, they have been duly noted. The Latin text followed is that of E. K. Rand in the Loeb Library edition (1918), which in turn is based largely upon R. Peiper's Teubner edition (1871). Acknowledgment must also be made of the German translation of E. Gothein (Zurich, 1949), which makes use of the text of W. Weinberger (Vienna, 1934).

J. J. B.

CONTENTS

BOOK I

*Meter I. Boethius bewails his
changed circumstances.*

"To pleasant songs my work was erstwhile given, and
bright were all my labors then; but now in tears to sad re-
frains am I compelled to turn. Thus my maimed Muses
guide my pen, and gloomy songs make no feigned tears
bedew my face. Them alone could no fear deter from accompanying me upon my way. They were the pride of my
earlier happy days; in my later gloomy days they are the
comfort of my fate. For hastened by unhappiness has old age
come upon me without warning, and grief has commanded
her years to lie upon me. White hairs are scattered untimely
on my head, and the skin hangs loosely from my worn-out
body. Happy is that death which thrusts not itself upon
men in their pleasant years yet comes to them at the oft-
repeated cry of their sorrow. Sad is it how death turns
away from the unhappy with deaf ear and cruelly refuses
to close the eyes that weep. Ill is it to trust to Fortune's
fickle bounty: while yet she smiled on me the hour of
gloom had well-nigh overwhelmed my head. Now, since
she has clouded over and changed her deceiving face, without scruple my life drags out its wearying delays. Why,
friends, did you so often puff me up, telling me that I was
fortunate? For he that is fallen low did never firmly stand."

*Prose I. Philosophy approaches Boethius: the
form of her appearance is allegorical.*

While I was pondering thus in silence and using my
pen to set down my tearful complaint, there appeared to
me standing overhead a woman whose countenance was
full of majesty, whose gleaming eyes surpassed in power
of insight those of ordinary mortals, whose color was full

1

of life, and whose strength was still intact though she was so full of years that by no means would it be believed that she was of our times. One could but doubt her varying stature, for at one moment she repressed it to the common measure of man, at another she seemed to touch with her crown the very heavens; and when she raised her head higher it pierced even the sky and baffled the sight of those who would look upon it. Her clothes were wrought of the finest thread by subtle workmanship into an indissoluble material. These she had woven with her own hands, as I learned afterwards from her own disclosure. Their color was somewhat dimmed by the dullness of long neglect, as happens likewise in the case of smoke-grimed death masks. On the border below was woven the symbol Π, on that above was to be read a Θ.[1] And between the two letters there could be seen degrees by which, as by the rungs of a ladder, ascent might be made from the lower principle to the higher. Yet the hands of certain rough men had torn this garment and had snatched such pieces as they could therefrom. In her right hand she carried books; in her left she brandished a scepter.

When she saw that the Muses of poetry were present by my couch giving words to my lamenting, she was stirred a while; her eyes flashed fiercely as she said: "Who has suffered these seducing mummers to approach this sick man? Never have they nursed his sorrowings with any remedies, but rather fostered them with poisonous sweets. These are they who stifle the fruit-bearing harvest of reason with the barren briars of the passions; they do not free the minds of men from disease but accustom them thereto. I would think it less grievous if your allurements drew away from me some common man like those of the vulgar herd, seeing that in such an one my labors would be harmed not at all. But this man has been nurtured in the lore of Eleatics and Academics. Away with you, Sirens, seductive

[1] Π and Θ are the first letters of the Greek words denoting Practical and Theoretical, the two divisions of Philosophy.

even to perdition, and leave him to my Muses to be cared
for and healed!"

Thus rebuked, that band cast a saddened glance upon
the ground, confessing their shame in blushes, and passed
forth dismally over the threshold. For my part, my eyes
were dimmed with tears, and I could not make out who
this woman of such commanding power was. I was amazed
and, turning my eyes to the ground, began in silence to
await what she would do next. Then she approached nearer
and sat down upon the end of my couch; she looked into
my face, heavy with grief and cast down with sorrow to the
ground, and raised her complaint about my mind's confusion in these words:

Meter II.

Philosophy acting as physician curing Boethius.

"Alas, how blunted grows the mind when sunk below
the overwhelming flood! Its own true light abandoned, it
strives to enter the darkness without. How often care when
fanned by earthly winds becomes a measureless bane. This
man, to whom once the sky was no limit, was wont to wan-
der into celestial paths, to watch the bright sun's rays, to
inquire into the cold moon's beams, and to calculate vic-
toriously the positions of all the planets which, moving through their different spheres, travel wandering
courses. . . .

His vision clouded

Prose II.

"But now," said she, "is the time for the physician's art
rather than for complaining." Then, fixing her eyes wholly
upon me she said: "Are you the man who, having been
nursed upon the milk of my learning and educated with
my food, had arrived at the power of a manly soul? Surely
I had given you such weapons as would keep you safe and
your strength unconquered, had you not thrown them
away. Do you know me? Why do you keep silence? Are
you dumb from shame or from amazement? I would it
were from shame, but I see that it is amazement that has

overwhelmed you." And when she saw that I was not only
silent but also utterly tongue-tied and dumb she put her
hand gently upon my breast and said: "There is no dan-
ger; he is suffering from drowsiness, a disease common to
minds that have been deceived. He has forgotten himself
for the moment but will quickly remember as soon as he
recognizes me. That he may do so, let me brush away from
his eyes the darkening cloud of things perishable." So saying, she gathered her robe into a fold and dried my tearful
eyes.

Meter III.

Then was night dispelled, the shadows left me, and my
eyes were restored to their former power. . . .

*Prose III. Boethius gains power
to address Philosophy.*

The clouds of grief having been scattered thus, I drew
breath again and engaged my mind in taking cognizance
of my physician's countenance. And so, when I had turned
my eyes and fixed my gaze upon her, I recognized my
nurse, Philosophy, in whose house I had been no stranger
ever since I had become a young man. And I asked her:
"Why have you, mistress of all virtues, come down from
heaven above to visit my lonely place of banishment? Is it
in order that you, as well as I, may be harried, the victim
of false charges?"

"Should I," said she, "desert you, my nursling, nor
share and bear my part of the burden which has been laid
upon you from spite against my name? Surely Philosophy
never allowed herself to let the innocent go upon their
journey unbefriended. Should I, terrified, fear calumnies, as
though they were a novel misfortune? Do you think this is
the first time that wisdom has been harassed by dangers
among men of shameless ways? Have I not even in ancient
days, before the time of my child, Plato, fought many a

mighty battle against the recklessness of folly? And, though Plato did survive, did not his master Socrates win his victory of an unjust death with me present at his side? After him, the herd of Epicureans and Stoics, and then others, all tried their utmost to seize the legacy of Socrates and to drag me off as their booty in spite of all my cries and struggles. They tore my robe which I had woven with my own hands and, having snatched away bits thereof, they departed thinking I had yielded myself to them entirely. But since at least a certain similarity to the way I bear myself could be discerned among these people, it was rashly supposed that some of them were actually my disciples, and they were done away with because the uninitiated crowd misjudged them. But if you have not heard of the exile of Anaxagoras, nor of the poison given to Socrates, nor of the tortures suffered by Zeno[2]—for these things, after all, did not happen in Rome—yet you may know of Canius, Seneca, and Soranus,[3] whose memory is still fresh and famous. For nothing else brought all these men to ruin but that, being instructed in my ways, they appeared at variance with the desires of unscrupulous men. Therefore you need not wonder if in this sea of life we are tossed about by storms from all sides, for we fulfill our calling best when we displease the worst. Though their band is indeed numerous yet it is to be contemned, for, undirected by any leading spirit, it is, hurried along at random by error alone, running riot everywhere. If this band, when warring against us, presses too strongly, our leader gathers her forces into her citadel while the enemy are occupied in plundering useless baggage. As they seize the most worthless things,

[2] Anaxagoras went into exile from Athens *circa* B.C. 450; Socrates was executed by the Athenian state, B.C. 399; Zeno of Elea is said to have been tortured by the tyrant of his native city *circa* B.C. 435.
[3] Julius *Canus* (so Seneca, *de Tranq.* xiv. 4-9) was put to death by Caligula *circa* A.D. 40; Seneca was driven to commit suicide by Nero, A.D. 65; Soranus was condemned to death by the same Emperor, A.D. 66.

^a we laugh at them from above, untroubled by the whole band of mad marauders and defended by that rampart to which riotous folly may not hope to attain.

Meter IV.

"He who has calmly reconciled his life to fate and set proud death beneath his feet, looking fortune good or bad in the face, can present a visage unconquered. . . .

Prose IV. Boethius complains to Philosophy of his sufferings after his just life.

". . . Why do you weep? . . . If you expect a physician's help, you must lay bare your wound."

Then I rallied my spirit until it was strong again, and said: "Does the savage bitterness of my fortune still need recounting? Does it not stand forth plainly enough by itself? Do not the very looks of this place strike you? Is this the library which you had chosen for yourself as a steadfast abode in my house, is this the room wherein you would often tarry with me expounding the philosophy of things human and divine? Was such my garb and my countenance when I probed with your aid nature's secrets, when you traced with a wand the stars' courses and shaped my habits and the rule of my entire life in accordance with the pattern of the celestial order? Are these the rewards I reap for obeying you? You yourself have sanctioned it when Plato said: 'Commonwealths would be blessed if they were guided by those who do make wisdom their study or if those who do guide them were to make wisdom their study.' [4] By the same man's mouth you taught that this was the binding reason why a commonwealth should be governed by philosophers, namely, that the helm of government should not be left to unscrupulous or criminal citizens lest they should bring corruption and ruin upon the good citizens. I was merely following these truths when I desired to practice in public administration what I had

[4] Plato, *Republic,* v. 473.

learned from you in quiet repose. You and God Himself, who has grafted you in the minds of philosophers, are my witnesses that never have I applied myself to any office of state save that I might help to realize what all good men strive to attain. This led to bitter and irreconcilable quarrels with evil men, and, as always happens when one follows one's own free conscience, to the relentless enmity of those in power, whom I disregarded in order to preserve justice. . . . You know that I, who have never been given to self-praise, declare this truthfully. For the secret value of one's conscience, that approves one's action, is lessened somewhat each time one receives the reward of fame by flaunting that action. But you see what end my innocence has received: in the place of the rewards for virtue rightfully mine I am suffering, wrongfully, the punishments for vice. . . . For my kindness I have received persecution, driven off as I have been from all my possessions, stripped of my honors, sullied in my reputation. I seem to see the intoxication of joy in the sin-steeped dens of criminals; to see every most abandoned man intent upon new schemes of false informations; to see good men lying prostrate beneath the terror of my crisis; to see every wicked man encouraged by impunity to dare any crime, indeed, by rewards to accomplish it; moreover, to see the innocent robbed not only of security but also even of making defense. So then I may well cry out:

Meter V.

". . . The hurtful penalty owed to crime falls upon the sinless, while depraved men rest at ease on lofty thrones and because of their unmerited lot crush under their hurtful heel the necks of virtuous men. . . ."

Prose V. Philosophy reassures him
and asks some probing questions.

When I had grieved thus in longdrawn pratings, Philosophy, moved not one whit by my complaints, with calm countenance said: "When I saw you in sorrow and tears I knew immediately that you were unhappy and in exile, but I knew not how distant was that exile until your speech betrayed it. Yet you have not indeed been driven but have wandered thus far from your native land; or if you prefer that you be considered driven then you have been driven by yourself rather than by another, for no one else could have done this to you. If you call to your mind what, really, is your fatherland, you know that it is not governed, as was Athens of old, by the multitude, but 'there is one Lord, one King,'[5] who rejoices in his citizens' great number, not in their banishment. To be guided by his reins, to subscribe to his justice, is the highest liberty. Are you ignorant of that most venerable law of your own state, by which it is established that no man who would set up a dwelling-place for himself therein may lawfully be banished? For anyone who feels safe within its protecting wall need not fear that he merits exile. Likewise any man who no longer wishes to dwell there no longer deserves such a home. Therefore it is rather the way you look than the looks of this place which disturb me.[6] Neither do I require the walls of your library, decked with ivory and glass, but rather a place in your mind, wherein I once placed, not books, but that which gives books their value: a store of thoughts from volumes of my own. As to your services to the common weal, you have spoken truly, indeed, but too modestly compared to your manifold exertions. . . .

Meter VI.

". . . God marks out the seasons, fitting each to its proper task; and whenever he has established a certain course of change he tolerates no confusion. Thus whatsoever betakes itself to headlong ways and leaves its fixed order has an unhappy ending.

[5] Homer, *Iliad* ii. 204f.
[6] Cf. Prose IV of this Book, p. 6.

Prose VI.

"First, then," she continued, "will you let me gain access to and find out the state of your mind by means of a few small questions, so that I may see what should be the method of treating you?"

"Ask," I replied, "what you think should be asked, and I will answer."

Then she said: "Do you think that this world is run by accidental and irregular chance, or do you believe that somehow it is ruled by reason?"

"I could," said I, "by no means believe that what is so certain and predictable could be run by irregular chance; I know that God the Creator presides over His work; and the day will never come that I will abandon this judgment as untrue."

"It is as you said," she continued. . . . "Yet, how strange! I am astonished that you, though holding firmly such a healthy opinion, should be so sick. But let us investigate more deeply. Though I cannot put my finger on it, I know that there is something lacking. Since you are not in doubt that the world is governed by God, tell me by what means you think that government is executed."

"I scarcely know the meaning of your question," said I, "much less can I reply to it."

"Was I wrong," said she, "to think that something was lacking, by which, as by a break in a fortified wall, this disturbing disease has crept into your mind? But tell me, do you remember what is the end of all things and the goal to which all Nature tends?"

"I have heard, to be sure," said I, "but grief has blunted my memory."

"But do you not know whence all things have their source?"

"Yes," I replied, "their source is God."

"And how can it happen that you, who know the origin of things, should not know their end? Yet such are the ways of these distractions, such is their power, that they can, indeed, move a man from his position, but they cannot entirely rend him asunder and deroot him, as it were, out of himself. But this question also I would have you answer: Do you remember that you are a man?"

"How could I not remember?" said I.

"Can you then explain what is a man?"

"Do you ask me whether I know that I am an animal, rational and mortal? This I know and confess myself to be."

And she said: "Don't you know yourself to be anything else?"

"No!"

"Now," said she, "I know another, and actually the greatest, cause of your sickness: you have forgotten what you are. Therefore I have found out to the full both the manner of your sickness and the means for restoring your health. Inasmuch as you have been confounded by forgetting what you are, you have been sorrowing that you are both exiled and robbed of your possessions. And inasmuch as you are ignorant of the end of all things, you imagine that worthless and wicked men are powerful and happy. Further, inasmuch as you have forgotten by what means the world is governed, you suppose that the turns of Fortune fluctuate with no guiding hand. These are causes enough not for disease alone but for death as well. But thanks be to the Author of health that your nature has not altogether left you. We have still the chief spark for your health's fire, namely, the true opinion of the world's governance, since you do believe that the world is subject not to random chance but to divine reason. Therefore have no fear: forth from this tiny spark your vital fire shall presently break. But since it is not yet time for firmer remedies and since it is agreed that it is the way of minds that, as often as they throw away true opinions, they become clothed with false, out of which is sprung a distracting darkness which confuses the true insight, I will try to lessen this darkness with gentle and moderate applications for a while, so that the shadows of deceiving passions may be dissipated and you may have power to perceive the brightness of the true light.

Meter VIII.

". . . If you wish to see the truth in undimmed light, choose the straight road, forsake joys and fear alike, put to flight vain hopes, and grant no place to grief. Where these distractions reign, the mind is clouded over and bound in chains."

BOOK II

*Prose I. Philosophy would prove that Boethius'
opinions and griefs are not justified in one of her
followers.*

After this she remained silent for a time and, when this
discreet silence had caused my thoughts to cease from
straying, she continued: "If I have thoroughly learned the
causes and condition of your sickness, you are being con-
sumed by a longing desire for your former fortune, and its
change, you imagine, has upset your peace of mind. . . .
You think that Fortune has changed towards you. You are
wrong. These are ever her ways; this is her very nature. She
has in your case maintained her proper constancy in the
very act of changing. Such was she when she smiled upon
you, mocking you with the blandishments of false happiness. You have discovered the ambiguous looks of this blind
deity. To others she is partially veiled; to you she is wholly
known. If you approve of her, make use of her ways and
make no complaining. If you are horrified by her perfidy,
treat her with scorn and thrust her and her pernicious play-
fulness aside. For she, who is the cause of your great sorrow now, ought to have been the cause of serenity. She, of
whom no man can ever be sure that she will not forsake
him, has forsaken you. Do you reckon as precious a happiness which will pass away? . . . Would you indeed attempt to stay the force of Fortune's turning wheel? O you
most dull-witted of all mortals, if Fortune begins to stand
still, she is no longer Fortune!

Meter I.

". . . Fortune heeds no wretch's cry, heeds no tears,
but wantonly mocks the sorrow which her cruelty has
caused. This is her sport, thus she proves her power: if in

the selfsame hour a man is raised to happiness, then cast down in despair, 'tis thus she shows her might.

Prose II. Philosophy shows how Fortune may plead her justification.

"Now I would argue a few matters with you using the words of Fortune herself, and do you therefore consider whether her demands are fair:

" 'Why, O man, do you daily accuse me, Fortune, with your complaints? What injury have I done you? What of your goods have I taken from you? Choose what judge you will and before him contend with me for the right to possess wealth and honors; and, if you can prove that these truly belong to any one of the mortals, readily will I grant that what you now seek to regain belonged to you. When Nature brought you forth from your mother's womb I received you naked and bare of all things, I cherished you with my resources and (that which now makes you impatient with me) I brought you up over-indulgently with favoring care and surrounded you with splendor and all the abundance that was mine to give. Now it pleases me to withdraw my hand; be thankful, as one that has lived upon another's property. You have no right to complain as though you had lost what was once your own. Why do you groan? I have brought no violence to bear. Wealth, honors and other things of that sort are within my province. They are my handmaids and know their mistress; they follow me in my comings and goings. Boldly will I say that, if these things, the loss of which you lament, had ever been yours, you would never have lost them at all.

" 'Am I alone to be prohibited from exercising my rights? Heaven may produce bright days, and then hide them beneath the shade of night. The year may deck the earth's countenance with flowers and fruits, and again wrap it with chilling clouds. The sea may now charm with smooth surface, now bristle with rough waves. Is the insatiable greed of man to bind me to a constancy alien to my ways? Herein lies my strength, this is my unending sport: I turn my flying wheel, and delight in changing top and bottom. Ascend to the top if you will, but on this condition, that you think it no unfairness to descend to the bottom when the rule of my game demands it. . . .

Meter II.

Philosophy?

" '. . . Savage greed swallows what it has gained and is wide open for more. What bridle will restrain within proper bounds headlong lust when, whetted by abundance of rich gifts, the thirst for possession burns? Never call we that man rich who is always trembling in haste and groaning for what he thinks he lacks.'

Prose III. Philosophy proceeds to justify Fortune in the balance of accounts with Boethius.

"If Fortune should thus defend herself to you," said Philosophy, "you would have nothing, I think, to say against her; or, if you should have any just defense for your complaining, you should put it forward. We will grant you the opportunity of speaking."

Material Boethius knows

Then I answered: "Those arguments have a fair form and are imbued with all the sweetness of Rhetoric and Music, but they delight only so long as one listens to them. The wretched have a feeling of their misfortunes too deep for these arguments. Wherefore when these sounds fall no longer upon the ear, deep-rooted misery again weighs down the spirit. . . ." [1]

Prose IV.

". . . Why, O Mortal men," she said, "do you seek happiness, which lies within yourselves, outside of yourselves? Error and ignorance confound you. I will briefly show you the pole on which the highest happiness turns. Is there anything you value more highly than your own

[1] Meter III. omitted entirely.

self? You will answer that there is nothing. Since then you have yourself, you are in possession of something which you will never wish to lose and which Fortune will never be able to take from you. And, that you may be assured that happiness does not consist of chance matters, consider this: if happiness is the highest good of a being endowed with reason and if that which can by any means be snatched away is not the highest good *excellent* (since that which cannot be taken away is always better), it is plain that the gifts of Fortune by their instability cannot ever lead to happiness. Furthermore, the man who is borne along by a felicity which may fall either knows that it may change, or he does not know it. If he does not know it, what bliss can there be in the blindness of ignorance? If he knows it, he must needs live in fear of losing what he does not doubt can be lost; wherefore such an ever-present fear does not permit him to be happy. . . . You, I well know, are persuaded that the mind of man is by no means mortal; this truth is planted in you by many proofs. Since then it is clear that fortuitous happiness is ended with the death of the body, it cannot be doubted that, if death can carry away happiness, the whole race of mortals sinks into wretchedness when at death's door. But if we know that many men have sought the fruits of happiness by means not only of death but also of sorrowful suffering, how then can momentary happiness make men happy when its end does not make them unhappy?

Meter IV.

"Let him who would cautiously build a lasting abode, firm enough to resist the blasts of the stormy wind and to defy the waves of the threatening sea, avoid the lofty mountain and the thirsting sands. The former is swept by all the might of the headstrong gale; the latter dissolve and will not bear up under a load. . . . *Fortune material happiness*

*Prose V. Philosophy examines more carefully
the value of things highly prized by men.*

"Now, since the first remedies of my reasoning are
sinking into you, I think that slightly stronger ones
should be used:

"If the gifts of Fortune did not fade or pass quickly
away, what is there in them which could ever be truly
yours or which would not lose its value when considered
and scrutinized?

"Are riches precious by virtue of their own nature, or
by virtue of your nature? . . . Does the gleam of gems
attract your eyes? But any excellence they have lies in
their own brilliance and belongs not to men; wherefore
I am amazed that men so strongly admire them. For how,
really, can they, which lack vital activity and bodily struc-
ture, seem beautiful to a rational and animated nature?
Although they be works of their creator and by reason
of their distinctiveness have a certain minor beauty, nevertheless they, ranked lower than your own excellence, in
no wise deserved your admiration. . . .

"Out of all these things which you reckon as your
wealth, not one can be shown to be really your own. . . .
If they are by nature beautiful what is that to you? For
they would have been pleasing of themselves even if cut
off from your possessions. They are not valuable by reason
of their having come into your property, but you have
desired to add them to your property because they seemed
valuable. . . .

"Is there then no good which belongs to you and is
inherent within you, so that you seek your goods in things
external and not a part of you? Have matters taken such a
turn that the animal whose reason gives it a claim to divinity
cannot seem beautiful to itself except by the possession of
inanimate trappings? Other creatures, indeed, are satisfied
with their intrinsic possessions; but you, made like God
through reason, take from the basest things the adornment

of your higher nature, and do not comprehend how greatly you thereby wrong your Creator. He intended the human race to be above all earthly things; you thrust down your dignity beneath the very lowest. For since the value of any thing is greater than the value of him to whom that thing constitutes his worth, then you who judge the vilest of things to give worth to you, assuredly place yourself lower than them in your own valuation; and this is indeed a just result. For such is the condition of human nature that it surpasses other classes only when it knows itself, but is reduced to a rank lower than the beasts when it ceases to know itself. For in other animals ignorance of self is natural; in men it is a moral defect. . . .

Meter V.

". . . Ah, who was he who first unearthed the mass of hidden gold, the gem that wished only to lie unfound, perilous prizes both? Who unleashed material wants? Pandora's box

Prose VI.

"What am I to say of offices and of authority, which you extol to heaven, not knowing what true dignities and dominion mean? What Aetnas, belching forth flames, what overwhelming flood could deal such ruin as these when they fall into the hands of evil men? I am sure you remember how your ancestors wished to do away with the Consular power, which had been the very foundation of liberty, on account of its holders' arrogance, just as your forefathers had too in earlier times expunged from the state the name of King on account of the same arrogance. But if, as rarely happens, offices are conferred upon upright men, what is pleasing about them other than the uprightness of their holders? Wherefrom it comes about that virtue is not honored by offices, but offices are honored by virtue. How true

"And yet what is the power which you seek and esteem so highly? O creatures of earth, do you not consider over whom you are set? . . . Can you impose any law upon a free spirit? Can you disturb the state of repose peculiar to a mind which acts in harmony with itself adhering to its own firm principle? When a certain tyrant thought that by torture he could compel a free man to betray the conspirators in a plot against his life, the latter bit off his tongue and spat it out in the former's face; thus the torture which was intended by the fierce one as matter for cruelty was turned by the philosopher into matter for high courage. . . .

"It is equally clear that those things are not by nature good which let themselves be attached to the worst men. And this indeed may the more worthily be held concerning all the gifts of Fortune, the more richly they are bestowed upon the most unscrupulous. Herein I think these facts must be considered: no one doubts that a man in whom one has seen bravery is brave, and it is manifest that whoever has swiftness is swift. In like manner music makes musicians, medicine medics, rhetoric rhetoricians. For everything does naturally its proper function, nor is it confused by the effects of contrary causes but spontaneously repels opposites. However, riches cannot extinguish insatiable avarice nor can power make master of himself the man whom vicious passions hold fast in unbreakable chains. And honors, when joined to dishonest men, so far from making them honorable, rather betray them and show them to be dishonorable.

Meter VI.

". . . Lofty power could not, could it, chasten depraved Nero's madness? Ah! heavy fate, how often is the sword of high injustice given where is already most poisonous cruelty!"

Prose VII. Philosophy discusses fame, 'that last infirmity of noble minds.'

Then said I: "You know that the ambitious striving after earthly things has had but little influence over me; but I

have chosen a field of activity so that my strength might
not grow old in inaction."

And she answered: "This is the one thing that can attract minds which indeed by nature excel but which not
yet have been led by perfection to the furthest bounds of
virtue: I mean the desire for glory and the reputation for
deserving well of one's country. Think then upon it and see
that it is but a slight thing of no weight.

"As you have learned from astronomical demonstra-
tions, the whole circumference of the earth is only a pin
point compared with the expanse of the heavens; that is to
say, when compared with the circle of the universe, it must
be reckoned as of no size at all. And of this tiny portion of
the universe there is barely a fourth part which is inhabited
by living beings known to us, as you have learned from the
proof of Ptolemy.[2] If from this fourth part you imagine
subtracted all that is covered by sea and marsh and all the
vast regions of thirsty desert, only the narrowest area is
left for human habitation. And you, so firmly restricted to
this infinitesimal point within a point, are thinking of pro-
claiming your fame and publicizing your name! What size
and magnificence can fame have when shut in by such close
and narrow limits? Futhermore, this narrow enclosure of
habitation is itself peopled by many races, which differ in
their language, in their customs, in their whole scheme of
living; and owing to difficulty of travel, diversity of speech,
and rarity of intercourse there cannot reach them the fame
even of cities, much less of individual men. Cicero himself
has written somewhere[3] that in his time the fame of Rome
had not yet crossed the mountains of the Caucasus, and yet
the Republic was then mature and formidable to the
Parthians and other nations in those parts. Do you see, then,

[2] Claudius Ptolemaeus, mathematician, astronomer and geographer of
Alexandria (*floruit* A.D. 121-151). Boethius translated some of his
works.
[3] Cf. *de Re Publica* vi. 20.

how narrowly limited must be the glory which you labor to extend more widely? Where the name of Rome cannot pass, will the fame of a Roman ever come? . . .

Meter VII.

"The mind that rushes headlong in its search for fame, thinking this its highest good, should look upon the spreading regions of the air, and then upon the confined tracts of the earth; it will feel shame that, though fame grow, it can never fill so small a circuit. . . .

Prose VIII.

"But, lest you think that I am waging inexorable war against Fortune, there are times when she, ceasing to deceive, deserves well of men: I mean when she reveals herself, unmasks her face and proclaims her ways. Perhaps you do not yet understand what I am saying. It's a strange thing that I'm trying to say, and for that reason I can scarcely explain my thoughts in words. I think that ill fortune is of greater advantage to men than good fortune. The latter is ever deceitful when, by a specious happiness, it seems to show favor; the former is ever true when, by its changes, it shows herself inconstant. The one deceives; the other edifies. The one, with a pretense of apparent goods, enchains the minds of those who enjoy them; the other, with a conception of happiness' brittleness, frees those minds. You see, then, that the one is blown about by winds, ever moving and ignorant of self, while the other is sober, ever prepared and prudent through the sustaining of adversity itself. Lastly, good fortune draws men from the path of true goodness with her blandishments; ill fortune in most cases draws men back to that path by force.

"And do you think that this should be reckoned among the least benefits of this harsh and frightful ill fortune, that she has disclosed the minds of your faithful friends? She has distinguished for you true and dubious friends, and at her departure has taken away her own and left you yours. At what a price would you have bought this benefit while you were unimpaired and, as you thought, fortunate! Now you indeed complain of your lost wealth, but you have found friends, the most precious kind of riches.

Meter VIII.

"... O happy race of mortals, if your hearts are ruled, as is the universe, by Love!"

BOOK III

Prose I.

When she had finished her song, its soothing tone left me spellbound, with ears alert in my eagerness to listen. Then after a while I said: "Greatest comforter of weary minds, how you have refreshed me with your deep thoughts and sweet singing, too! No longer shall I doubt my power to meet the blows of Fortune. Not only do I no longer fear those remedies which you did recently tell me were too sharp, but I am longing to hear them and zealously request them."

Then said she: "I knew it when you laid hold of my words in rapt attention, and I was waiting for that frame of mind in you, or, more truly, I effected it myself. The remedies which remain are indeed bitter to the taste but sweet to the inner man that receives them. You say you are eager to hear, but how ardently would you be burning if you knew whither I am attempting to lead you!"

"Whither is that?" I asked.

"To the true happiness," she replied, "of which your soul, too, dreams, but which it cannot behold as it really is because your sight is occupied with shadow."

Then said I: "I pray you show me what that true happiness is, and quickly."

"I will do so willingly for your sake," said she, "but first I shall attempt to picture in words and give form to something which is better known to you, in order that, when it has been understood and you turn your eyes to the other side, you may recognize the form of true happiness." [1]

[1] Meter I omitted entirely.

22

Prose II. Philosophy discusses 'the highest Good.'

Then, having lowered her gaze for a little while and, as it were, having retired into the innermost recess of her soul, she began in this manner: "The labor involved in the multiple pursuits of mortal men brings them much anxiety; but though they go forward by different paths they strive to reach one end, which is happiness. And that is that good which, once attained, leaves nothing further to be desired. It is the highest of all goods and contains within itself whatever is good; for if it lacked any good it could not be the highest Good, since something desirable would be left out. Therefore happiness is clearly a state which is made perfect by the union of all goods and which, as I said all men seek to achieve, albeit by diverse paths. For there is implanted by Nature in men's minds a desire for the true Good, but error leads them astray to false goods.

"Now, some men believe that the highest Good is to lack nothing and so are at pains to possess abundant riches. Others consider the true Good to be that which is most worthy of admiration and so strive to attain to places of honor, thereby to be respected by their fellow-citizens. Some determine that the highest Good lies in the highest power and so either wish to reign themselves or try to cleave to those who do reign. Others think that renown is the greatest Good and so hasten to propagate a glorious name by the arts of peace or of war. But the majority measure the fruits of the Good in terms of joy and gladness and regard the happiest man as one abandoned to pleasure. . . .

"Do they seem to err who endeavor to want nothing? Surely there is nothing which can make happiness so complete as a state of abundant supply of all good things, which needs nothing further and is sufficient unto itself. Surely, too, those are not mistaken who think that what is best is also most worthy of reverence and respect. For that can be no cheap or contemptible thing which nearly all men aim and strive to attain. And surely power must be enumerated among goods; for can that be judged a weak and strengthless thing which consistently surpasses all other things? Again, is renown of no importance? But this fact cannot be laid aside: whatever is most excellent seems to be most famous also. It is purposeless to mention that happiness is not unpleasant and sad nor subject to grief and trouble, since even in the smallest matters the object is to find that which it is a delight to have and enjoy. These, then, are what men wish to obtain: riches, honors, empires, glories, and pleasures; and they desire them because they imagine that thereby they will find sufficiency, veneration, power, fame and joy. It is the Good, therefore, which men seek by such diverse pursuits, and it is easily shown how great is the force of Nature, seeing that, though opinions be varying and discordant, all agree in choosing the Good as the end.

Meter II.

"I would to pliant strings set forth a bright song about how almighty Nature turns her guiding reins, with what laws her providence keeps safe the immense universe, binding and tying each and all with cords that cannot be loosed. . . .

Prose III. Philosophy shows the vanity of riches.

". . . Consider whether men can reach their appointed end, happiness, by those ways by which they suppose they will attain thereto. For if riches, honors and the like do bring about a state in which no good seems to be lacking, then let us acknowledge that some men do become happy through the acquisition of these things. But if these things cannot perform their promises since each one of them fails to provide many other good things, then clearly a specious happiness is apprehended in them. . . ." [2]

---

[2] Meters III-VII and Prose passages IV-VII omitted entirely.

Prose VIII. All these vanities are actually harmful.

"Now, there is no doubt that these so-called roads to happiness are only byways which cannot lead any one whither they profess to lead. I shall very briefly show you with what great evils they are entangled. Would you attempt to heap up money? You will have to tear it away from its owner. Would you appear brilliant by means of honors? You must kneel before their dispenser and, in your desire to surpass others in honor, you must stoop to the humility of begging. Do you long for power? You will be subjected to your subjects' wiles and exposed to dangers. Do you seek fame? You will be drawn to and fro along rough paths and lose all security. Would you spend a life of pleasure? Yet who should not spurn and reject servitude to so vile and frail a thing as the body? How petty are the aims of those who place before themselves the pleasures of the body, how uncertain is the possession of such!. . .

Meter VIII.

". . . Men in their blindness are content not to know where lies hidden the Good which they desire. They are immersed in earthly things and therein seek that which dwells above the starlit heavens. . . .

Prose IX. Philosophy begins to examine true happiness.

"So far," she continued, "it has sufficed to set forth the essence of false happiness and, if you clearly understand that, the next order of business is to show what true happiness is."

"I do see," said I, "that sufficiency cannot come through wealth, nor power through kingdoms, nor veneration through high office, nor renown through glory seeking, nor joy through bodily pleasures."

"And have you grasped the reasons why this is so?"

"I seem to look at them as through a narrow chink,

but I would prefer to learn them more openly from you."

"The reason is to hand: human error divides that which is by nature simple and indivisible, and thus turns its truth and perfection into untruth and imperfection. Tell me, do you think that a state which lacks nothing can lack power?"

"Of course not," I replied.

"You are right. . . . Therefore sufficiency and power have one and the same nature."

"So it seems."

"And do you think a state of this sort is contemptible or, on the contrary, worthy of all veneration?"

"The latter case, without a doubt," said I.

"Then let us add veneration to sufficiency and power, so that we may consider these three as one."

"We must add it, if we wish to confess the truth."

"What now?" she said. "Do you think that this whole is something obscure and ignoble or something renowned with all glory? Consider it thus: it has been conceded that this state lacks nothing, includes every power, and is most worthy of veneration; could it then lack renown and be unable to attain it without thereby appearing to be somewhat contemptible?"

"I cannot but admit," said I, "that it has great renown too."

"Consequently we must rank renown with the other three."

"Yes, we must," said I.

"Then that which lacks nothing from outside, which includes every power by reason of its own strength, which has veneration and renown, must clearly be most joyful too."

"I cannot imagine," said I, "from what quarter sorrow would creep into such a state; wherefore it must be granted that, if its other characteristics remain in existence, it is full of gladness."

"Then it follows by the same reasoning that though

sufficiency, power, renown, veneration, and pleasure differ
in name, they do not differ at all in substance."

"They cannot," I replied.

"What, therefore, is simple and single by nature is
divided by human depravity; and while man tries to gain
a part of that which has no parts, he fails to obtain both the
portion, which cannot exist by itself, and the whole, after
which he does not strive."

"How so?" I asked.

"One man seeks riches to escape penury," she said,
"but he takes no thought of power, prefers to be base and
unknown, and even deprives himself of many natural
pleasures lest he part with the riches he has gathered. But
in this way not even sufficiency befalls him, while power
forsakes him, anxiety molests him, cheapness demeans him,
and obscurity conceals him. Another man desires power
only; he scatters his wealth, despises pleasures, rejects
honors which involve no power, and sets no value upon
glory. You see how many things such a man lacks. Sometimes he even goes without necessities, sometimes he feels
the pinch of anxieties and, since he cannot rid himself of
these, he loses the power which he sought above all. The
same argument may be applied in the case of offices, of
glory, and of pleasures. For since each one of these is the
same as the rest, any man who seeks one without the others
gains not even that which he desires."

"But what," I asked, "if a man desires to obtain all these
things simultaneously and at once?"

"Then he indeed wishes for the sum of happiness. But
will he ever find that in these things, which we have shown
cannot supply what they promise?"

"Never."

"Therefore happiness is not to be looked for among
these things which are believed to supply the separate por-
tions of what is sought."

"Admittedly," I replied, "nothing could be more
plainly true."

"Now then," said she, "you have both the essence of false happiness and the reasons why it is false. Turn your attention in the opposite direction and you will quickly perceive the true happiness which I promised to show you."

"Why," I said, "this would be perfectly clear even to a blind man; you showed it to me a little while ago while you were trying to make clear to me the reasons why false happiness is false. For if I mistake not, that is the true and perfect happiness which makes a man sufficient, powerful, venerated, renowned and joyful. And (for I would have you know that I have looked into this matter rather deeply) I realize without a doubt that that which can truly yield any one of these states, seeing that they are all one, is fully-perfected happiness."

"O my pupil!" she exclaimed, "I will think you happy in this opinion, if only you add one thing."

"What's that?" I inquired.

"Do you think there is anything in our mortal and perishable affairs which could grant a state of this sort?"

"No," said I, "as I think you have shown beyond need of further proof."

"These then seem to yield to mortals either mere images of the true Good or certain imperfect goods; they cannot confer the true and perfect Good."

"I agree," I said.

"Since, then, you have seen what is the true happiness and what are the false imitations thereof, it now remains for you to learn where you may seek this true happiness."

"I have been waiting for that impatiently for a long time," said I.

"But," said she, "since divine aid must be implored in small things as well as in great (as my pupil Plato says in his *Timaeus*,) [3] what do you think we must do to merit finding the place of that highest Good?"

"The Father of all must be invoked," I replied, "for when that is not done no undertaking is rightly begun."

[3] 27 C.

"You are right," she said, and at once she sang the following:

Meter IX. Philosophy invokes God's guidance.

"Thou who dost govern the universe with everlasting law, Founder of earth and heaven who biddest time roll on from age to age, forever firm Thyself yet giving movement unto all things, . . . grant that we may behold the fount of the Good; grant that, when the light has been discovered, we may set upon Thee the soul's unblinded eyes. Hurl asunder the heavy clouds of this material world, and shine forth in Thy splendor! For Thou art to the pious a serene and tranquil rest; to discern Thee is our aim. Thou art our beginning, our progress, our guide, our way, our ending.

Prose X. Philosophy discourses on the union of the Highest Good with God.

"Since, then, you have seen the essence both of the perfect and of the imperfect good, I think I should now point out wherein lies the perfection of happiness.

"To discuss this problem, we must first inquire whether any good of the kind as you have defined it can exist as something real, so that we are not deceived by an empty mental picture to which nothing real truly corresponds. Yet there can be no denial that such a good exists and that it is the very source, so to speak, of all other goods. Now everything which is judged to be imperfect is judged to be so because of some defect. Wherefore if a particular thing is imperfect in any specific respect, the existence of some other thing perfect in this respect is necessary. For if the perfection did not exist, one could not even imagine from what the so-called imperfect could arise. For Nature does not take its start from what is defective and imperfect, but proceeding from the consummate and absolute, it gradually degenerates into what is lower and weaker. If, then, as we have shown above, there is a certain imperfect felicity based on a fragile good, one cannot doubt that there is also a permanent and perfect happiness."

"That is quite surely proved to be true," said I.

"Now consider," she said, "where this perfect happiness dwells. That God, the Author of all things, is good, is a universally accepted notion of mankind and in no need of proof. For since nothing better than God can be imagined, could anybody doubt that He, than whom there is nothing better, is good? And, actually, reason proves that God is good by showing that even the perfect Good must reside in Him. For if the perfect Good did not reside in Him, He could not be the Author of all things. For there would have to exist something which, by possession of the perfect Good, would be more excellent than He is, and this something would obviously precede Him in rank and time, for it is already obvious that perfect things are of earlier origin than imperfect things. Wherefore, lest the series be prolonged *ad infinitum*, it must be allowed that the most high Deity is full of the most high, the perfect, Good. But as we have determined that the perfect Good is the true happiness, it must also be that said true happiness resides in the most high God."

"I accept that," said I; "it cannot be in any way contradicted."

"But please see to it that you prove faultlessly and uncontradictably that, as we have said, the highest God is most full of the highest Good."

"How?" I asked.

"Do not presume that God, the Father of all things, whom we hold to be filled with the highest Good, either has received this Good from without or possesses it by nature in such a way that you might consider Him, its possessor, and the happiness possessed as being distinct and different. For if you were to think that the Good has been received from without, you could also think that that which gave it is more excellent than that which received it; yet we have correctly conceded that God is the most excellent of all things. And if you think that the highest Good is in Him by His nature but as something different from Him, then, since we speak of God as the Author of all things, who could imagine by whom such different things as God and the Good could have been united? Finally, that which is different from something else is not the same as that from which it is understood to differ. Wherefore that which is by its nature different from the highest Good is not itself the highest Good—which it is not lawful to think of God, than whom, it is agreed, nothing is better. Absolutely nothing in the world can have a better nature than its origin; wherefore I would conclude, according to the truest reasoning, that that which is the origin of all things is in its own substance the highest Good."

"Most truly," I said.

"But it has been conceded that the highest Good is happiness?"

"Yes," I said.

"Therefore," she said, "it must be confessed that God is Happiness itself."

"I cannot gainsay what you premised before," said I, "and I perceive that this follows necessarily from those premises."

"Look then," she said, "whether the same proposition is not proved more strongly by the following argument: there cannot be two different highest Goods. For it is clear that where there are two different goods the one cannot be the other; wherefore neither one can be the perfect Good while each is wanting to the other. And that which is not perfect is manifestly not the highest; therefore, if two things are the highest Good, they can by no means be different. Further, we have concluded that both God and happiness are the highest Good; therefore the highest Deity must be identical with the highest happiness."

"No conclusion," said I, "could be truer in fact or stronger in theory or worthier of God."

"Over and above this," she said, "let me give you a corollary, such as geometricians are wont to do when they wish to derive a deduction from the propositions they have demonstrated. Since men become happy by attaining happiness, and happiness is identical with divinity, it is plain that they become happy by attaining divinity. And as men become just by attaining justice and wise by attaining wisdom, so by the same reasoning they become God-like by attaining divinity. Every happy man, then, is God-like; but, while there is nothing to prevent as many men as possible from being God-like, only One is God by nature: men are God-like by participation."

"This conclusion or corollary or whatever you prefer to call it is fair and very precious," said I.

"Yes, but nothing is more beautiful than this, too, which reason leads us to add to what we have proved."

"What is that?" I asked.

"Many things—[sufficiency, power, honor, etc.]—seem to be included in what we term 'happiness.' Do all these things together join to form the one body of happiness, each one of them being, so to speak, a different member of that body? Or does one of them in itself contain the whole substance of happiness, so that the others stand merely in some relation to this one?"

"I wish," said I, "that you'd clear up this matter yourself by the enunciation of the particulars."

"Do we not," she asked, "hold that happiness is a good?"

"Yes," I answered, "the highest Good."

"But," she said, "one may add this quality of happiness, namely 'goodness,' to all the others. For the highest sufficiency, the highest power, veneration, fame, and pleasure are also judged to constitute happiness. What then? Do all these things together—sufficiency, power, and the rest—constitute the Good in the sense that they are members of the body of happiness or of the Good? Or are sufficiency, power and the rest all related to the Good as to their common center?"

"I understand," I answered, "what you propose to investigate, but I desire to hear what you decide."

"Learn thus my decision in this matter: if these were all members of the one body, happiness, they would differ individually. For it is the nature of parts that, each differing from the others, they make up one whole. But sufficiency, power, and all the rest have been shown to be one and the same. Therefore they are not members, for otherwise happiness would appear to be joined together out of one member, which cannot happen."

"That is quite certain," said I, "but I'm waiting for what's to come."

"It is plain that the others are to be referred back to the Good. For sufficiency is sought because it is judged to be good; power likewise; and we may infer the same thing about veneration, fame, and pleasure. The Good, then, is the sum and substance of all the things we desire and the reason why we desire them. For what has within itself no real or even pretended good cannot ever be sought. On the other hand, those things which are not by nature good but nevertheless seem to be so are sought as though they were truly good. Wherefore goodness may rightly be believed to be the sum and substance of everything we desire and the reason for desiring it. Indeed, that on account of which anything is desired seems to be the main object of that desire. For example, if a man wishes to ride for the sake of his health, he desires not so much the motion of riding as the effect of health. As, therefore, sufficiency, power, fame, etc., are sought for the sake of the Good itself, it, rather than they, is desired by everyone. But we have agreed that these other things are desired for the sake of happiness; happiness then is, just like the Good, that for the sake of which everything else is sought. Wherefore it is clear that the substance of the Good and of happiness is one and the same."

"I do not see why anyone would dissent."

"And we have shown that God and true happiness are one and the same."

"Yes," said I.

"Therefore we may safely conclude further that God is none other than the Good itself."

Meter X.

"Come hither, all who are the prey of passions, bound by their ruthless chains, those deceitful passions which dwell in the minds of men. Here shall you find rest from your labors, here a haven lying in tranquil peace, open to receive within itself all the miserable on earth. . . ." [4]

Prose XII. Philosophy shows that God rules the universe for the highest Good.

". . . This world," she continued, "you thought a little while ago must without doubt be guided by God."

"And I think so now," said I, "nor will I ever think there is any doubt about it." . . .

Then she said: "Since you are of this opinion I feel there is left for me only a little trouble before you may, with happiness in your possession, safely return home. But let us look more closely at what we have asserted. Have we not reckoned sufficiency to be one aspect of happiness, and agreed that God is Happiness itself?"

"Yes indeed."

"Wherefore," said she, "God needs no external aids in governing the universe; otherwise, if He had any such need, He would not have complete sufficiency."

"That of necessity follows," I said.

"Then He arranges all things by Himself alone."

"Without doubt He does," said I.

"And God has been proven to be the absolute Good."

"I remember," I said.

"Then He arranges all things through the Good, if indeed He arranges them through Himself, who, we have agreed, is the Good. And He is as it were the helm and the rudder by which the ship of the universe is preserved stable and uncorrupted."

[4] Prose XI and Meter XI omitted entirely.

"I most strongly agree," I said; "and I foresaw a little while ago that you would say this, though I had slight qualms."

"I believe it," said she, "for now you are making your eyes scan the truth more watchfully. But what I am going to say is no less plain to the sight."

"What's that?" I asked.

"Since," she replied, "God is rightly believed to steer all things by the helm of the Good and since all things have a natural inclination to hasten to the Good, can there be any doubt that beings having a will of their own are also guided and that they turn themselves of their own accord to their disposer's will, agreeing with, and obedient to, the helmsman?"

"It must be so," I replied, "nor would this government appear happy if it were a yoke upon the rebellious rather than the salvation of the obedient."

"Then there is nothing which, so long as it remains faithful to its nature, attempts to oppose God?"

"Nothing," said I.

"But," she asked, "if anything does make the attempt, will it ever have any success at all against Him who, as we have conceded, is by the right of His happiness the most powerful?"

"Certainly not," I replied.

"Then there is nothing which has either the will or the power to resist this highest Good."

"I think not," said I.

"Therefore," she said, "it is the highest Good that is ruling all things inescapably and guiding them gently and without compulsion."

Then said I: "How greatly am I delighted, not only with the things that have been proved by the strongest of arguments, but still more with the very words which you employ in order that at last the folly which afflicted me sorely may be put to shame!"

"You have heard," she said, "in mythology how the

giants rebelled against heaven. They, too, then, as was fitting, were being 'ruled inescapably and guided gently' by the highest Good in their endeavor!—but maybe we should let the reasons for and against this conclusion conflict. Perhaps from such a friction some spark of truth may leap forth."

"As you judge best," said I.

"Nobody," she said, "would doubt that God is all-powerful."

"At any rate," said I, "no sane man would doubt it."

"Being all-powerful, then," she said, "there is nothing which He cannot do."

"Nothing," said I.

"Can God therefore do evil?"

"By no means," I answered.

"Then," said she, "evil is nothing, and does not exist, since He who can do everything cannot do it."

"Are you toying with me?" I asked. . . .[5]

---

[5] Meter XII omitted entirely.

BOOK IV

Prose I. They discuss the possibility of evil in God's world.

. . . "Herald of true light," I said, "what you have said up to now has been clear, seeming not only inspired as one contemplates it but also invincible through your arguments. And, although I had recently forgotten these things owing to grief over the injustices I suffered, nonetheless you have spoken of things not entirely unknown to me previously. But the main cause of my grief is the fact that, though there exists a good Governor of the world, evil can exist at all and even go unpunished. I would have you consider how strange this fact is in itself. But there is an even stranger fact attached hereto: while ill-doing reigns and flourishes, virtue not only lacks its reward but is even trampled underfoot by the wicked, and it, not villainy, is punished. No one could wonder and complain enough that such things should happen under the rule of a God who, while all-knowing and all-powerful, wills good alone."

Then she said: "Yes, it would be most horrible, monstrous, and infinitely amazing if it were as you think. It would be as though in the well-ordered house of a good master the cheapest vessels were cared for while the precious became defiled. But it is not so. If our former conclusions remain unshaken, God Himself, of whose government we now speak, will teach you that the good are indeed always the powerful and the evil always the abject and weak; that vice never goes unpunished nor virtue unrewarded; that felicity always falls to the good and misfortune to the evil; and many similar truths which, when your complaints have been set at rest, will confirm you most solidly in your opinion. . . .

Meter I.

"Yea, flying wings are mine to scale the heights of heaven; when these the mind has donned, swiftly it loathes and spurns the earth. . . ."

Prose II. Philosophy argues that the good are powerful, the bad are weak.

Then I cried: "What vast things you promise, nor do I doubt that you can fulfill them. I ask you only that you not hold me back with delays, now that you have excited me."

"First, then," she said, "you may recognize that power is ever present to the good, while the wicked are devoid of all strength: the one follows from the other. Good and bad are opposites. If therefore the power of goodness be proved, the weakness of evil is plain; and if the instability of evil is made manifest, the stability of goodness is proved. But to gain more abundant credibility for my opinion I shall proceed to confirm my argument by first the one and then the other of the two paths.

"It is agreed that there are two things upon which depends the performance of every human action: will and power. If one of these be lacking, nothing can be effected. For, if the will be lacking, a man does not even undertake that which he has no desire to perform, while, if the power be lacking, the will is exercised in vain. Wherefore, if you see a man wish for what he will never gain, you cannot doubt that he lacks the power to do what he would."

"That is plain beyond doubt," said I.

"But, if you see a man gain what he wishes, can you doubt that he has the power?"

"No."

"Now, wherein a man has power, he is strong; wherein he has not power, he must be counted weak."

"Yes," said I.

"Do you remember," she asked, "we deduced from our

earlier reasonings that every inclination of the human will, though following diverse paths, aims with eagerness towards happiness?"

"I remember," I replied, "that that also was proved."

"Do you recall that happiness is the absolute Good, so that, when happiness is sought, the Good is desired by all?"

"I need not recall that," I answered, "since I hold it fixed in my mind."

"Then all men, good and bad alike without distinction, instinctively seek to arrive at the Good?"

"Yes," I replied, "that follows necessarily."

"But it is certain that the good become so by the attainment of goodness."

"Yes."

"Then the good attain what they seek?"

"So it seems."

"But if evil men were to attain the Good, which they seek, they could not be evil."

"That is so."

"Since, then, both classes seek the Good, which the good attain but the evil do not, can there be any doubt that the good are powerful, while the evil are weak?"

"Whosoever doubts that," I replied, "cannot judge either the nature of things or the logic of arguments."

"Again," she continued, "if there are two persons before whom the same goal is placed in accordance with their nature and one of them, by functioning naturally, strives for and attains the goal, while the other one, unable to function naturally, can, by a method contrary to nature, merely imitate the successful person without actually fulfilling his task, which of these two do you judge to be the more powerful?"

"Although I can guess what answer you want," I said, "I wish to hear the question put more clearly."

"You won't deny," she asked, "that the motion of walking is natural to mankind?"

"No, I won't," I answered.

"And is not this the function natural to the feet?"

"Yes," I replied.

"If, then, one man walks, being able to use his feet, while another whose feet do not function normally tries to walk by using his hands, which of these two may justly be thought the more powerful?"

"Weave me other riddles," I exclaimed, "for no one would doubt that a man who can exercise his natural functions is more powerful than he who cannot."

"Yet in the case of the highest Good, which object is placed equally before good and bad men, good men seek it in the natural way through virtue, while bad men strive to attain it through various forms of lust, which is not the natural way to attain it. Or do you think otherwise?"

"Not at all," I replied, "and the deduction which follows is also plain. For it must be, from what I have already conceded, that the good are powerful, the bad weak."

"Your anticipation is correct," she said, "and (as doctors are wont to hope) this is an indication of an improved condition now fit to withstand disease. In fact, since I see that you are very prompt to understand I will multiply my arguments one upon the other. See how great is the weakness of those wicked men who cannot even attain that to which their natural inclination leads, almost compels, them. And how much worse off would they be if they were deprived of this great and all but invincible aid of nature's leading the way! Think what a powerlessness possesses these men. The objectives which they seek and cannot achieve are not light or trifling, but they fail in the very sum and crown of all things and cannot accomplish that for which they labor night and day in wretchedness. Yet herein the strength of good men is conspicuous. For just as you would consider him a most powerful walker who could advance on foot until he arrived at a point beyond which there lay no path for further progress, so you must consider that man most powerful who reaches a point beyond which there is nothing to be desired. From this it follows—and this is the other side of the argument—that evil men are those whose whole strength has deserted them. For why do they abandon virtue and pursue vice? From ignorance of what is good? Yet what is weaker than the blindness of ignorance? Or do they know what they ought to pursue but are thrown off the straight road by passions? Then they must be weak too in self-control if they cannot struggle against vice. Or do they knowingly and willingly desert the Good and stoop to evil? But they lose in this way not only power, but existence altogether. For those who abandon the end common to all things which exist must in the same measure cease to exist. It may seem strange to some that I maintain that evil men, though constituting the majority of mankind, do not exist; yet it is true. For while I do not deny that evil men are evil, I do deny that they 'are,' in the pure and full sense of the term 'existence.'

"You may say, for instance, that a corpse is a dead man, but you cannot call it simply a man; in like manner I grant that wicked men are bad, but I cannot allow that they exist in the full sense. For that thing exists which keeps its proper rank in the order of being and preserves its nature; when it falls away from this nature it relinquishes also its existence, which is grounded in its nature. . . .

Meter II.

"Kings you may see sitting aloft upon their thrones, gleaming with purple, hedged about with grim weapons, threatening with fierce glances, their hearts heaving with passion. If any man take from these proud lords their outward covering of empty honor, he will see that they bear inside secret chains. For the heart of one is filled by lust with the poisons of greed, while towering rage lifts up its waves and lashes the mind of another; or gloomy grief holds them both as weary captives, or by slippery hopes are they tortured. Thus, when you see one head laboring beneath so many tyrants, you may know he cannot do as he would, for by harsh taskmasters is the master himself oppressed.

Prose III. The good and the evil have their own rewards.

"Do you see, then, in what a slough crimes are involved, and with what glory honesty shines forth? It is hence plain that its own reward is never lacking to virtue, nor punishment to vice. For we may justly think that the reward of every act that is performed is the same thing as the object for which it is performed; for example, on the racecourse the crown for which the runner contends lies as the reward. But we have shown that happiness is the absolute Good for the sake of which all acts are performed. Therefore the absolute Good is, as it were, the reward proposed for all human acts. And good men cannot be deprived of this, for indeed a man who lacks the Good will no longer correctly be called a good man; wherefore virtuous conduct is never left without its own reward. However wildly, then, the wicked rage, the wise man's crown will never fall or wither. For the wickedness of others does not take away from virtuous souls the glory which is theirs. Now, if one were to rejoice in something received from others, then could some one else, even he who conferred it, carry it off; but, since virtue grants to each his own reward, he will lack his reward only when he shall have ceased to be virtuous. Finally, since every reward is sought after only because it is believed to be a good, who would judge that the man who possesses goodness is without his reward?

"And what reward is this? The fairest and greatest of all. Remember that corollary which I laid down as a precept a little while ago[1] and reason thus therefrom: since happiness is the absolute Good, it is clear that all good men are made happy by virtue of the very fact that they are good. But we agreed that happy men are God-like. Therefore this is the reward of the good, which no time can

[1] Pp. 31-32 above.

ravage, no man's power lessen, no man's wickedness obscure: they become God-like.

"Since this is the case, no wise man can be in doubt about the punishment inseparable from wickedness. For since good and evil, and likewise reward and punishment, are opposites, the reward which we see come to the good must correspond precisely to the punishment which comes to the evil. As, therefore, honesty is itself the reward of the honest, so wickedness is itself the punishment of the wicked. . . .

"As goodness alone can raise a man above the level of humanity (to God-likeness), so evil of necessity lowers beneath that level those whom it has ejected from their human status. The result is that you cannot hold him to be a man whom you see transformed by vices. If a thief and a robber burns with greed of other men's possessions, you say he is like a wolf. Another ferocious man is forever working his restless tongue at lawsuits: you will compare him to a hound. Does another delight in creeping up from ambush with hidden guile upon men? He is like a fox. Does another roar, giving license to his temper? He would be reckoned as having a lion's heart. Does another flee and tremble in terror when there is no cause to be afraid? He would be considered deerlike. If another is dull and lazy, does he not live the life of an ass? Another, whose aims are inconstant and lightly changed, is in no wise different from the birds. If another is immersed in foul and filthy lusts, he is kept down in a swine's slough. Thus it is that he who deserts goodness ceases to be a man and, since he cannot change his condition to God-likeness, turns into a beast. . . .[2]"

Prose IV.

". . . What I am about to say . . . follows from what has been concluded."

"What's that?" I asked.

[2] Meter III omitted entirely.

"That wicked men are happier when they pay the penalty than when they evade the hands of justice.[3] I am not now urging what may occur to anyone, namely, that depraved habits are corrected by punishment and lead back towards the right through fear of penalty and that an example is hereby given to others to avoid all blameworthy acts. Even if no account be taken of the corrective power or the exemplary value of judgment, I *still* think that from another point of view the wicked who go scot-free are the more unhappy."

"And what point of view is there other than these?" I asked.

She said: "We have allowed, have we not, that the good are happy, but the bad miserable?"

"Yes," I replied.

"Then," said she, "if some good be added to the misery of any man, is he not happier than the man whose state is misery pure and simple, without the admixture of any good whatsoever?"

"So it seems," I replied.

"What if there were added some further evil beyond those by which this same wretch who lacked all good things was made miserable? Should he not be reckoned far more unhappy than the man whose misfortune is lightened by some share of good?"

"Of course," I replied.

"Yet it is manifestly just that the wicked be punished, manifestly unjust that they escape unpunished."

"Who would deny that?"

"But," said she, "no one will deny this either, that all that is just is good and that, on the other hand, all that is unjust is bad."

"That's clear," said I.

"Therefore, the wicked, when punished, have something good added to their lot, to wit, the punishment itself, which is good by reason of its justice; and they like-

[3] Cf. Plato, *Gorgias*, 472ff.

wise, when unpunished, have a certain further evil, to wit, the impunity itself, which you have allowed to be an evil by reason of its injustice."

"I cannot deny that."

"Then the wicked are far more unhappy when they are unjustly unpunished than when they are justly punished." . . .[4]

Prose V. Boethius still feels dissatisfaction with the world's government.

Hereupon I said: "I see how both happiness and misery lie placed in the deserts of men, both good and bad. Still, I am sure that there is good and evil also in what generally happens to people as the result of good or bad fortune. . . . I wonder greatly . . . why punishments for crimes overwhelm the good while the bad receive the rewards for virtues. I long to learn from you what is the reason for such unjust confusion. I should wonder less if I could believe that the general confusion resulted from accident and chance. But now the fact of God's guidance increases my amazement. He often distributes pleasant things to the good and harsh things to the bad and, on the other hand, sends hardships to the good and grants the wishes of the bad. Unless a reason for this is discovered, how would it seem to differ from accident and chance?"

"It is not surprising," she answered, "if something be thought confused and in random order when the reason behind this order is unknown. But do not doubt that all things are rightly done, since a good Governor orders the universe, even though you are ignorant of the reason behind so great an ordering.

Meter V.

". . . The causes of some things lie ready at hand to discern, of other things lie hidden and trouble men's hearts. At all things which time brings forth infrequently and of

[4] Meter IV omitted entirely.

a sudden the fickle herd is amazed. But let the cloudy errors of ignorance depart, and straightway these shall cease to appear marvelous."

Prose VI. Philosophy discusses Providence and Fate.

"That is true," I said; "but since it is your kind office to unravel the causes of hidden matters and to explain reasons veiled in darkness, I beg of you, put forth your decree and expound all to me, because this wonder most deeply stirs my mind."

Then she said, smiling a bit: "Your question calls me to the greatest of all matters and a full answer is well-nigh impossible. For it is a problem of the kind that, if one doubt is cut away, innumerable others crop up like the Hydra's heads, nor will there be any limit unless one restrains them by the most lively mental fire. For this question involves the problems (you can judge for yourself their weight) of the simplicity of Providence, of the course of Fate, of unforeseen chance, of divine foreknowledge and predestination, and of the freedom of the will. Yet, since it belongs to your cure to know of these things also, I will attempt to touch upon them somewhat, though we are hemmed in by a short space of time. But if you enjoy the delights of song you must wait a while for that pleasure, while I, connecting link to link in due order, forge for you the chain of arguments."

"As you will," said I.

Then, as though beginning anew, she spoke as follows: "Every kind of change, no matter whether it be the generation of new things or the development of all things mutable, draws its cause, order, and form from the immutability of God's mind. This mind, in the calm fortress of its own simplicity, establishes the mode of governing things. This mode is called Providence when it is considered in the very purity with which it is conceived by God, but it was called Fate by the ancients when viewed with reference to the objects it moves and orders. It will easily be understood that Providence and Fate are very different if the mind examines the meaning of each. For Providence is the divine reason itself, which arranges all things and dwells in the supreme Director of all. Fate, however, is that disposition inherent in mutable things through which Providence binds everything to its decrees. For Providence embraces all things in the same way, no matter how different and limitless they are. On the other hand, when all these things have been assigned individually to their places, forms, and times, Fate sets them in motion; so that this evolution of the temporal order, unified in the foresight of the divine mind, is Providence, while this same unity, developed and evolved in time, is called Fate.

"Though Fate and Providence are not the same, still the one depends on the other, for the order of Fate proceeds from the simplicity of Providence. Just as an artificer, conceiving in his mind the form of the thing to be made, goes to work and accomplishes in accordance with the order of time that which he had foreseen simply and instantaneously; so by means of His Providence does God dispose by a single and unchangeable act all that is to be done. But these same things which He has disposed He executes by means of Fate in manifold ways and in time. Whether, therefore, Fate is exercised through certain divine spirits attendant upon Providence or whether its thread is woven through the service of a soul or of all nature, or through the motions of the stars in heaven, or through the angels' virtue, or through the demons' varied ingenuity, or through some or all of these, one thing is certain: Providence is the immutable and simple design of all things that are to come to pass, while Fate is the mutable bond and the temporal order of those things which are disposed to come to pass by the divine simplicity. Everything, therefore, which is subject to Fate is also subject to Providence, to which Fate itself is subject. . . . As, therefore, discursive reasoning is related to insight, as that which becomes is

related to that which is, as time is related to eternity, . . .
thus is related the ever-changing course of Fate to the un-
changing simplicity of Providence. This course (of Fate)
. . . constrains the actions and fortunes of men by an
unbreakable chain of causes; and, since this chain proceeds
at its inception from an immutable Providence, the causes
also must themselves be immutable. For thus are things best
governed if the simplicity resident in the divine mind puts
forth an order of causes which may not change. This order
restrains, by its own unchangeableness, changeable things
which might otherwise be in random flux. Wherefore, although to you, who are not strong enough to comprehend
this order, all things may appear confused and upset, nevertheless all things are disposed by their own proper measure
directing them to the Good. For there is nothing which
comes to pass for the sake of evil, not even at the hands of
evil men themselves, of whom it has been abundantly shown
that distorted error averts them from the Good they seek.
Much less does the order which proceeds from the center
of the highest Good ever deflect from its origin." . . .[5]

[5] Meters VI-VII and Prose passage VII omitted entirely.

BOOK V

Prose I. Philosophy discusses the nature of "chance."

Here she made an end and was for steering the conversation to certain other matters for treatment and development. Then said I: ". . . I am learning in fact what you stated in word a while ago: the question of Providence is bound up in many others. I would ask you whether you think that chance exists at all, and what you think it is."

Thereupon she said: "I am eager to fulfill my promise and to open for you the way which you may return home. But these things, though very useful to know, are nevertheless rather removed from our proposed path, and we must be careful lest you, wearied of side trips, be not strong enough to complete the main journey."

"Have no fear at all of that," said I; "it will be restful for me to know these things in which I delight so much. At the same time, since every side of your argument has stood firm with unshaken credit, let there be nothing ambiguous about its sequel."

Then she said; "I will gratify you," and began to speak as follows: "If anyone define chance as the outcome of random motion produced by no sequence of causes, I am sure there is no such thing and consider it an empty, meaningless word, even if we refer by it to some actual event. For what place can be left for any random happening, seeing that God keeps everything in order? It is a true statement that nothing comes out of nothing. None of the ancients ever denied it; and, though they did not derive this axiom from thinking about the operating principle but from thinking about the matter operated upon, they laid it down, so to speak, as the foundation for all their reasoning about Nature. Now if something were to arise from no cause, it would appear to have arisen out of nothing. Since this is impossible, then chance also, of the sort such as we just defined, cannot exist."

"Then," I asked, "is there nothing which can justly be called chance or accident? Or is there something which, although unknown to common people, these words do suit?"

"My philosopher, Aristotle," she replied, "defined it in his *Physics*[1] briefly and well-nigh truly."

"In what way?" I asked.

"Whenever," she replied, "something is done with one intention but something else, other than what was intended, results from certain causes, that is called chance; as, for instance, if a man, breaking ground for the purpose of cultivating a field, finds a mass of buried gold. Such a thing is believed to have happened by chance, but not from nothing, for it has its own causes whose unforeseen and unexpected coincidence seems to have brought about a chance. For, had not the cultivator dug the ground and had not the depositor buried the money in that particular spot, the gold would not have been found. These then are the reasons for that profitable accident, which came about from the meeting and confluence of causes, not from the intention of the actors. For neither he who buried the gold nor he who worked the field intended that the gold should be found, but, as I said, it was a coincidence that the one happened to dig where the other had buried. Chance therefore may be defined as an unexpected result from the coincidence of certain causes in matters done for some other purpose. The order of the universe, advancing with inevitable sequence, brings about this coincidence and confluence of causes. This order emanates from its source, which is Providence, and disposes all things in their proper time and place.

Meter I.

". . . Chance, which seems to flow onward without rein, bears the bit and makes its way by rule."

[1] Book II, Chapter IV.

Prose II. Philosophy asserts the existence of free will.

"I have listened," said I, "and agree that it is as you say. But is there any freedom for our wills in this series of cohering causes, or does the chain of Fate bind the very movements of our minds as well?"

"There is free will," she replied, "nor could there be any reasoning nature without it. For any being that, by its nature, can use reason has a power of discernment with which it can judge any thing. By itself, therefore, it distinguishes between objects to be shunned and objects to be desired. Now, everyone seeks what he judges to be desirable, and flees what he deems should be shunned. Wherefore all who have reason have also within themselves freedom of desiring and refusing. But I do not lay it down that this freedom is equal in all beings. Heavenly and divine substances have at hand an acute judgment, an uncorrupted will, and the power to effect their desires. Human spirits must be the more free the more they maintain themselves in the contemplation of the divine mind, less free when their attention is distracted towards material things, and less free still when they are tied to their earthly members.[2] Indeed, the last stage is mere slavery, wherein the spirit is delivered over to vices and has fallen away from the possession of its reason. For when the mind's eye turns from the light of the highest truth to what is lower and less lucid, it is soon dimmed by the clouds of ignorance and becomes turbid through ruinous passions; by yielding and consenting to these passions, men increase the slavery which they have brought upon themselves and become in a certain way captive through their own freedom. But all these things are known in the sight of that Providence which foresees all things from eternity and disposes each according to its own deserts as predestined.

[2] Cf. Plato, *Phaedo*, 80Bff.

Meter II.

". . . As to the Creator of this great sphere, no masses of earth can block His vision as He looks over all; night's cloudy darkness cannot obstruct it. In one stroke He sees in His mind all that has been, that is, and that is to come. Since He alone can see all things, one may call Him the true Sun."

Prose III. Boethius cannot reconcile God's foreknowledge with man's free will.

Then I said: "Behold, again I am plunged into yet more difficult doubt."

"What is it," she asked, "although I already have an idea of what your trouble consists?"

"There seems," I replied, "to be such incompatibility between the existence of God's universal foreknowledge and that of man's free will. For, if God foresees all things and can in no wise be mistaken, then that which His Providence foresees as going to happen must result necessarily. Wherefore, if from eternity He foreknows not only men's deeds but also their designs and wishes, there will be no free will; for there can neither be any deed done nor wish formed except such as the infallible Providence of God has foreseen. For, if matters could ever be so turned as to result otherwise than was foreseen, His foreknowledge of the future would never be certain but would rather be uncertain opinion, a thing which I deem impious to attribute to God. And, further, I cannot approve of that argument by which some men think they can solve this knotty problem: they say that a future event does not come to pass for the reason that Providence has foreseen it, but rather, on the contrary, since it is about to come to pass it cannot be hidden from divine Providence. In that way necessity is taken away from the events foreseen and attributed to the act of foreseeing, so that it is not necessary that what is foreseen should actually happen but necessary that those things which are going to happen be also foreseen; as though, indeed, our problem was: What is the cause of what? Is God's foreknowledge the cause of the necessity of the future, or is the necessity of the future the cause of God's foreknowledge? Whereas we actually strive to prove this, that, howsoever this causal relation be ordered, the event of the things foreknown is necessary, even if foreknowledge itself does not seem to induce this necessity of the event into things to come. For, if a man is seated, then the opinion which conjectures that he is seated must be true and, conversely, if the opinion that the man is seated is true, then he must necessarily be seated. There is therefore necessity in both cases: in the former the opinion must be true and in the latter the man must be seated. However, he is not seated because the opinion is true, but rather the opinion is true because his being seated has preceded it. . . .

"It is manifest that we should reason in like manner concerning Providence and future things. For, even if these are foreseen because they are about to happen, and do not happen because they are foreseen, it is nevertheless necessary both that what is about to happen should be foreseen by God and that what has been foreseen should happen as it was foreseen, and this last alone is enough to destroy free will. Yet how preposterous it is for us to say that the event of temporal affairs is the cause of eternal foreknowledge! Moreover, to hold that God foresees future things because they are about to happen is nothing else than to think that what has happened in the past is the cause of that highest Providence. Besides, just as when I really know that something exists it must needs exist, so also when I really know that something is about to come to pass it must needs come to pass. Thus it follows that the event of a thing foreknown is inevitable. Finally, if any one believes something which is actually not so, he has no knowledge but a fallacious opinion, a thing far removed from scientific truth. Wherefore, if any future thing is future in such a way that its event is not sure or necessary, how can it possibly be known beforehand that it will occur? For, just as knowledge itself is unmixed with falsity, so also that which is conceived by it cannot be otherwise than it is conceived. That is the reason why knowledge does not lie, because each matter must be just as knowledge understands it to be. What then? How does God foreknow uncertain future things? For, if He thinks inevitable the event of such things as may possibly not occur, He is mistaken; and this it is impious for us to think, or even to utter. But if He judges these uncertain future events to be as uncertain as they actually are, i.e., if He knows only that they may or may not occur, then one can hardly speak of fore*knowledge*, for He would know nothing certain and definite. Or wherein does it differ from that ridiculous prophecy of Tiresias: 'Whatever I say shall either be or not.' [3] How, too, would God's Providence be better than man's opinion, if like mankind He judges uncertain those things whose event is uncertain? But if there can be nothing uncertain in that most certain Font of all things, then those things which He has firmly foreknown as things which are going to happen will certainly happen. Wherefore there exists no liberty for human designs and actions. For the divine mind, foreseeing all things without the error of deception, restricts and binds each one of them to one single outcome. Once this has been admitted, it is plain what a destructive effect such an admission must have for all human affairs. In vain are rewards and punishments proposed for the good and the bad, for there are no free and voluntary actions of the mind to warrant them. And what we now judge most fair will prove to be most unfair in all respects, namely, to punish the wicked or reward the upright, since not their own will but the fixed necessity of the future forces them to do either good or evil. There will no longer be such things as virtues or vices but merely an indiscriminate mixture of merit and/or guilt. And nothing more criminal than this could be imagined: since the whole order of things proceeds from Providence and nothing is left to human designs, it follows that our vices as well as our

[3] Horace, *Satires* II. v. 59.

virtues must be referred to the Author of all good things. Hence there is no reason to hope for or to pray against anything, for what could any man hope for or pray against when all that can be desired is merely a link in an inflexible chain of events? Thus there will be taken away that sole intercourse betwixt God and man, namely, the right of prayer. . . .

Meter III.

"What cause of discord is it that breaks the bonds of concord here? What heavenly power has set such strife between two truths? For, though apart each brings no doubt, yet will they not be linked together. Or is there no discord between these truths, and do they stand forever sure side by side? . . ."

Prose IV. Philosophy tries to show how fore-knowledge and free will may be reconciled.

Then she said: "This is an ancient plaint concerning Providence, strongly argued by Marcus Tullius when dealing with divination,[4] and a matter about which you yourself have made long and frequent inquiries. But hitherto neither of you have developed it with enough diligence and precision. The reason why the solution of this problem has always remained hidden is the fact that the step-by-step process of human reasoning cannot attain to the act of simple insight which divine foreknowledge is. If our minds could somehow operate this latter way, there would be no doubt left at all; I will try to make this clear after I have explained your difficulties. Tell me why you think ineffectual the argument of those who solve the problem thus: they think that free will is not in any way shackled by foreknowledge, because they hold that foreknowledge is not the cause of the necessity in future things. Whence do *you* draw your evidence for the necessity of future things if not from the fact that things foreknown cannot but come

[4] Cicero, *de Divinatione* ii.

to pass? If, then, as you yourself admitted a while back, foreknowledge imposes no necessity upon future things, what could possibly change voluntary acts into necessary ones? Let us assume for the sake of argument, so that you may see what follows, that there is no foreknowledge at all. Then, under the circumstances thus assumed, are the events resulting from free will bound by necessity?"

"Of course not."

"Now, let us assume that foreknowledge exists, but imposes no necessity upon things; then, I think, the same freedom of will shall be left, intact and absolute.

" 'But,' you will say, 'although foreknowledge does not establish any necessity for the event of future things, yet foreknowledge is a sign that they will necessarily come to pass.' It would plainly follow that the event of future things would be necessary even if there were no foreknowledge. For a sign merely points at what is; it does not bring into being that which it points out. Wherefore it must first be proved that nothing happens but of necessity before it can be demonstrated that foreknowledge is a sign of this necessity. Otherwise, if there is no necessity, foreknowledge cannot be a sign of that which does not exist. . . . Now how can it possibly be that things which are foreseen as about to happen should not take place? For apparently we refuse to believe that those events whose occurrence Providence has foreseen might actually not occur; nevertheless we choose to believe that such events, even when they actually occur, did not have to happen by a necessity inherent in their nature—which fact you may easily gather from the following example:

"We see many things occur before our eyes, for instance, those things which charioteers are seen to do when they drive and turn their chariots, and in like manner other things. Does any necessity compel any one of these things to happen as it does?"

"By no means, for all skills would be of no effect if all things took place by compulsion."

"Therefore, since these things have no necessity for occurring at the moment they happen, they cannot, before they actually occur, happen with necessity in the future. Wherefore there are certain things about-to-come-to-pass whose occurrence is absolutely free from any necessity. For I believe no one would say that the things which are done in the present were not about-to-be-done in the past, before they were done. Thus these foreknown events occur freely. Just as knowledge of present things imposes no necessity upon them while they are being done, so foreknowledge does not impose any necessity upon future things. 'But,' you will say, 'this itself is dubious, whether there can be any foreknowledge of those things which do not occur necessarily.' To you a 'foreknowledge of things which do not occur necessarily' implies a contradiction; you believe that if they are foreseen the necessity (of occurrence) follows, that without this necessity there can be no foreknowledge, that all knowledge is always knowledge of something certain, and that, if things which will not occur necessarily are foreknown as necessary, we are not dealing with the truth of knowledge but with the obscurity of opinion. For you believe that to judge anything as other than it is in fact is far removed from the integrity of true knowledge.

Philosophy discusses the various grades of cognition.

"The cause of your error is that every man believes that all the things he knows come to his knowledge solely through their own nature and through a force inherent in them. But the opposite is true. For everything which is known is comprehended not according to its own force but rather according to the faculty of those who comprehend it. Let me make this plain by a brief example: the roundness of a body is recognized by sight in one way, and by touch in another way. Sight, remaining at a distance, takes in the whole body at once with all its diverging radii, while touch, clinging and conjoined, as it were, to the sphere, comprehends the roundness of the body as it passes inch by inch over the actual circumference. Likewise sense, imagination, reason, and insight all behold a man differently. For sense considers his figure as it is impressed on his body, while imagination considers the figure by itself without the body. Reason goes further than this: by contemplating only the universal aspects it investigates the species itself, which is represented in particular specimens. Higher still is the view of insight: reaching beyond the sphere of the material universe it beholds with the pure vision of the mind the Idea of Man in its simplicity.

"Herein the chief point for our consideration is this: the higher power of comprehension includes the lower, but the lower can in no wise raise itself to the higher. For the senses are capable of comprehending nothing but matter; imagination cannot look upon universal species; reason cannot grasp the simple Idea; but insight seems to look down from above and, after having perceived the Idea, judges everything patterned after this Idea in the same way in which it comprehends the Idea itself, which can be known by no other faculty. For insight knows the universal grasped by reason, and the immaterial figure visualized by imagination, and the material object perceived by the senses, making use neither of reason nor of imagination nor of the senses but seeing with one grasp of the mind all things in their Idea, so to speak. Reason, too, when it views a universal, makes no use of the imagination or the senses, and yet it comprehends the objects both of imagination and of sensation. For it is reason which defines a universal resulting from its own mode of conception like this: man is a two-footed, rational animal. Though this is a universal notion, everybody knows that what reason thus considers not by an act of the imagination or of the senses but by an act of rational conception is a thing accessible to imagination and sense. Likewise, although imagination takes its beginning of seeing and forming figures from the senses, still without their aid it surveys each sensible thing not with a sensory but with an imaginary faculty of distinguishing. Do you see, then, that in the act of knowing all subjects employ their own faculty rather than that of the objects known? And this is only reasonable for, since every judgment formed is an act of the person who judges, every man must of necessity perform his own operation with his own and not another's faculty.

Meter IV.

"In days of old the Stoic School produced men who, seeing dimly as in old age, could believe that the feelings of the senses and the imagination were but impressions on the mind from external bodies, just as it was once the custom to impress with swift-running pens letters upon the surface of a waxen tablet which bore no previous marks. But if the mind with its force can develop nothing by its own exertions, if it does but lie passive and subject to the marks of outer bodies, if it reflects like a mirror merely the shallow reflections of other things, whence thrives there in the soul an all-seeing power of knowledge? What is the force that sees the individual parts or which classifies the facts it knows? What is the force which gathers up the parts it has distinguished and, electing a varied route, now rears its head among things on high, now descends to things below and then, returning to itself, refutes falsehood with truth? This is a more efficient, a far mightier cause than that which merely receives the impressions of matter. Yet the passive reception does come first, rousing and stirring all the strength of the mind in the living body. When the eye is smitten with a light or the ear is smitten with a voice's sound, then is the mind's energy aroused and, thus moved, calls upon like appearances, such as it holds within itself, fits them to external signs, and mingles the figures of its imagination with those which it has stored within.

Prose V. Philosophy discusses the difference be-
tween human reason and divine insight.

"If, with regard to perceiving physical objects, although the qualities projected from without affect the sensory organs and although the body's passive reception, preceding the mind's energetic action, calls forth to itself the
mind's activity and arouses the hitherto quiescent ideas
within; if, I repeat, with regard to perceiving physical objects, the mind does not passively receive impressions from
said objects but of its own power judges the reception de-
pendent on the body, how much less do those beings which
are free from all affections of the body follow in their judgment external objects, but rather they release the independ-
ent actions of their minds. For this reason many different
manners of cognition have fallen to widely different substances. The senses alone, destitute of any knowledge but
their own, have fallen to those living beings which are in-
capable of motion, like the shellfish of the sea and other low
forms of life which live by clinging to rocks; while imagination has fallen to animals with the power of motion, who
seem to be affected by a desire to seek certain things and
to avoid others. But reason belongs to the human race
alone, just as insight is God's alone. . . .

"Suppose then that sensation and imagination oppose
reasoning, saying that those universals which reason pre-
tends to contemplate do not exist, arguing that what is comprehensible to the senses and imagination cannot be universal; that therefore either the judgment of reason is true
and nothing comprehensible exists or (since reason knows
full well that there are many objects comprehensible to the
senses and imagination) the conceptions of reason are
empty because it holds the individual thing comprehensible
to the senses to be something universal. If reason were to
respond that it does, indeed, perceive the objects of sense
and imagination from a universal point of view; that sense
and imagination, on the other hand, cannot aspire to knowl-

edge of universals since their manner of cognition goes no
further than bodies and figures; and that in matters of
knowledge it is best to trust to the stronger and more
nearly perfect judgment—if such a trial by debate occurred
should not we, who have the power not only to reason but
also to imagine and perceive with the senses, approve reason's cause rather than the others'? We are dealing with
a similar situation when human reason supposes that the divine insight cannot contemplate future things except as it
(the human reason) conceives them. For you argue thus:
'If there are some things which do not occur necessarily and
certainly, then it cannot be known in advance with cer-
tainty that these things will actually occur; therefore there
can be no foreknowledge of these things for, if we believe
that they can be foreknown, then everything happens by
necessity.' If we, however, who partake of reason, could
also share that power of judgment which is proper to the
divine mind, we would think it most fitting that, just as we
have decided that the senses and imagination should yield to
human reason, so the latter should submit itself to the divine mind. Let us therefore raise ourselves, if we can, to
that height of the loftiest intelligence. For there reason will
see what she cannot intuit on her own, i.e., how foreknowledge sees distinctly and certainly even those things which
occur without necessity and how such foreknowledge is
not mere opinion but rather the simplicity of the highest
knowledge, unencumbered by any finite bounds.

Meter V.

"In what varied shapes do living beings move upon the
earth! Some with extended body sweep through the dust
and employ their strength to make a continuing furrow;
some flit here and there on light wings that fan the breeze,
and float through vast tracts of air in their easy flight.
Others delight in planting their footsteps on the ground and
in striding across green fields or through forests. Though
all these you see moving in different shapes, yet all have

their faces inclined along the ground, and this drags down-
ward and dulls their senses. Alone of all, man lifts up his
head on high and stands in easy balance with the body
upright, and looks down to spurn the earth. If you be not
too earthly through evil folly, the pose is as a lesson. Your
glance is upward and you carry high your head, and thus
your search is heavenward. Then lead your mind, too, upward, lest while the body is higher raised the mind settle
lower toward the earth.

*Prose VI. Philosophy explains that God's insight
views all things in their eternal design, while
human reason can see them only from a temporal
viewpoint.*

"Since then, as we have just now shown, everything
that is known is apprehended not according to its own nature but according to that of the knower, let us examine
now, so far as we lawfully may, what is the state of the divine substance, so that we may be able to learn also what its
knowledge is. The common opinion, according to all men
living, is that God is eternal. Let us therefore consider what
eternity is, for this will make clear to us at the same time
the divine nature and the divine knowledge. Now, eternity
is the complete possession of an endless life enjoyed as one
simultaneous whole; this will appear clearer from a com-
parison with temporal things. For whatever is living in time
proceeds in the present from times past to times future; and
nothing existing in time is so constituted as to embrace the
whole span of its life at once, but it has not yet grasped to-
morrow, while it has already lost yesterday. In this life of
today you are living in no more than a fleeting, transitory
moment. And so it is with everything that is subject to the
condition of time: even if it should never have begun and
would never cease to be—which Aristotle believed of the
universe—even if its life were to be co-extensive with the

infinity of time, yet it could not rightly be held to be
eternal. For, even granted that it has an infinite lifetime, it
does not embrace this life as a simultaneous whole; it does
not now have a grasp of the future, which is yet to be lived
through. What is rightly called eternal is that which grasps
and possesses simultaneously the entire fullness of an unending life, a life which lacks nothing of the future and has
lost nothing of the fleeting past. Such a being must necessarily always be its whole self, unchangingly present to itself, and the infinity of changing time must be as one present
before him. Wherefore they are mistaken who, hearing that
Plato thought this world had no beginning in time and
would have no end, think that in this way the created universe is co-eternal with the Creator.[5] For to pass step by step
through an unending life, a process ascribed by Plato to the
universe, is one thing; to embrace simultaneously the whole
of an unending life in one present, an act manifestly peculiar
to the divine mind, is quite another thing. And, further, God
should not be regarded as older than His creations by any
quantity of time but rather by the peculiar quality of simplicity in His nature. For the infinite motion of temporal
things tries to imitate the ever present immobility of His
life, does not succeed in copying or equalling it, sinks from
immobility into motion, and falls from the simplicity of the
present to the infinite stretch of future and past; and since
it cannot possess its life completely and simultaneously it
seems to emulate, by the very fact that it somehow exists
forever without ceasing, what it cannot fully attain and
express, clinging as it does to the so-called present of this
short and fleeting moment, which, inasmuch as it bears a
certain resemblance to that abiding present, makes those to
whom it comes appear to exist. But, since this present could

[5] Boethius speaks of people's "hearing that Plato thought," etc.,
because this was the teaching of some of his successors at the Acad-
emy. That Plato himself thought otherwise may be seen, e.g., from
Timaeus 38B, where time is said to have come into being along with
the universe.

not be abiding, it took to the infinite journey through time, and so it has come to pass that, by journeying on, it continues that life the fullness of which it could not grasp by staying. Thus if we would apply proper epithets to these subjects we would say, following Plato, that God is eternal, while the universe is perpetual.

"Since, then, every judgment comprehends the objects of its thought according to its own nature, and since God has an ever present and eternal state, His knowledge also, surpassing every temporal movement, remains in the simplicity of its own present and, embracing infinite lengths of past and future, views with its own simple comprehension all things as if they were taking place in the present. If you will weigh the foresight with which God discerns all things, you will rightly esteem it to be the knowledge of a never fading instant rather than a foreknowledge of the 'future.' It should therefore rather be called *pro*vision than *pre*vision because, placed high above lowly things, it looks out over all as from the loftiest mountain top. Why then do you demand that those things which are translucent to the divine mind's light be necessary if not even men make necessary the things they see? Because you can see present things, does your sight impose upon them any necessity?"

"Surely not."

"Yet, if one may not unworthily compare the human present with the divine, just as you see certain things in this, your temporal present, so God sees all things in His eternal present. Wherefore this divine foreknowledge does not change the nature or properties of things: it sees things present to its contemplation just as they will turn out some time in the future. Neither is there any confusion in its judgments of things: with one glimpse of the mind it distinguishes what will happen necessarily and what will happen non-necessarily. For example, when you observe at the same time a man walking on the earth and the sun rising in the sky, although you see both sights simultaneously, nevertheless you distinguish between them and judge that the one is moving voluntarily, the other necessarily; in like manner the intuition of God looks down upon all things without at all disturbing their nature, yet they are present to Him and future in relation to time. Wherefore it is not opinion but knowledge grounded in truth when He knows that something will occur in the future and knows as well that it will not occur of necessity. If you say at this point that what God sees as about to happen cannot but happen and that what cannnot but happen happens, and you pin me down to this definition of necessity, I will confess a matter of the firmest truth but one which scarcely any one save a contemplator of the divine can reach: i.e., I shall answer that one and the same future event is necessary with respect to God's knowledge of it but absolutely free and unrestrained when it is examined in its own nature.

"For there are two kinds of necessity. One is simple: for instance, it is necessary that all men are mortal. The other is conditional: for instance, if you really know that a man is walking, he must be walking. For what a man really knows cannot be otherwise than it is known to be. But the conditional kind of necessity by no means implies the simple kind, for the former is not based on the very nature of the thing called necessary but on the addition of an 'if.' For example, no necessity compels a man who is walking of his own accord to proceed, though it is necessary that, *if* he is walking, he should be proceeding. In the same way, if Providence sees any thing as present, that thing must be, though it has no necessity of its own nature; and, of course, God sees as present those future things which come to pass through free will. Therefore free acts, when referred to the divine intuition, become necessary in the conditional sense because God's knowledge provides that condition; on the other hand, viewed by themselves, they do not lose the perfect freedom of their nature. Without doubt, then, all things which God foreknows do come to pass, but certain of them proceed from free will. And these free acts, though they come to pass, do not by actually occurring lose their proper nature, because of which, before they come to pass, they could also not have come to pass. . . .

" 'But,' you will say, 'if it is within my power to change my mind I can make Providence void, for I may change what she foreknows.' To this I will answer that you can indeed change your mind but, since Providence truly sees in her present that you can change it, whether you will change it, and whither you may change it, you cannot avoid the divine foreknowledge any more than you can avoid the glance of an eye which is present, though you may by your free will turn yourself to various different actions. You will then say, 'Will the divine foreknowledge be altered by my own disposition, so that when I choose now one thing, now another, it too will seem to undergo alternations in its own cognition?' By no means; for the divine insight precedes the future and recalls it to the one present of its own proper cognition. It does not alternate, as you suppose, between this and that in its foreknowledge, but it is constantly preceding and grasping with one glance all mutations. This presence of comprehending and witnessing all things is not based on the actual occurrence of future events but on God's own peculiar simplicity—which fact also resolves that problem which you posed a little while ago when you said that it is shameful to maintain that our future acts are the cause of God's knowledge. For this power of knowledge to take cognizance, with one ever present glance, of all things has itself determined for each thing its mode of existence and owes nothing more to future things. Since this is so, mortal man's freedom of judgment remains inviolate and, because his will is free from any necessity, the laws which propose rewards and punishments are not unjust. God is the ever prescient spectator of all things, and the eternity of His vision, which is ever present, runs in unison with the future nature of our acts, dispensing rewards to the good, punishments to the evil.

Hopes are not vainly put in God nor prayers vainly offered which, if they be right, cannot be ineffective. Therefore turn from vice, cultivate virtue, raise your heart to legitimate hope, direct humble prayers to the heavens. If you will only take notice and not dissemble, a great necessity for righteousness is laid upon you, since you live under the eyes of a Judge who discerns all."